Puns
Spooken
Here

Also by Richard Lederer

Adventures of a Verbivore
Anguished English
Basic Verbal Skills (with Phillip Burnham)
The Bride of Anguished English
The Circus of Words
Comma Sense (with John Shore)
Crazy English
The Cunning Linguist
Fractured English
The Giant Book of Animal Jokes (with James Ertner)
Get Thee to a Punnery
Have Yourself a Punny Little Christmas
Literary Trivia (with Michael Gillcland)
A Man of My Words
The Miracle of Language
More Anguished English
The Play of Words
Pun & Games
The Revenge of Anguished English
Sleeping Dogs Don't Lay (with Richard Dowis)
The Word Circus
Word Play Crosswords (with Gayle Dean)
Word Wizard
The Write Way (with Richard Dowis)

Happy Halloween! 2010

Puns
Spooken Here

WORD PLAY FOR

HALLOWEEN

Richard Lederer

Illustrations by
Jim McLean

Wyrick & Company
CHARLESTON

First Edition
09 08 07 06   10 9 8 7 6 5 4 3 2 1

Published by
Wyrick & Company
An imprint of Gibbs Smith, Publisher
P.O. Box 667
Layton, UT 84041

Orders: 1.800.748.5439
www.gibbs-smith.com

Designed by Mary Ellen Thompson, TTA Design
Printed and bound in the United States of America

Library of Congress Cataloging-in-Publication Data

Lederer, Richard.
Puns spooken [sic] here / Richard Lederer ; illustra-
tions by Jim McLean.—1st ed.
p. cm.
ISBN 0-941711-79-X
1. Puns and punning. 2. Halloween—Humor. I. Title.

PN6231.P8L45 2006
818'.602—dc22

2006013411

To Stan Kegel,
a true servant of punnery.

Contents

�֎

1

A Feast of Halloween Puns

You may well have heard the seasonal prey upon words "What do you call an empty hot dog?" Answer: A hollow weenie.

But you may not have realized how capacious is the tricky treat bag of Halloween puns. There's something about the lore of Halloween that inspires tour de farces at the highest level of punnery. What this book will offer you is a veritable Bill of Frights.

Punnery is largely the trick of compacting two or more ideas within a single word or expression. Punnery challenges us to apply the greatest pressure per square syllable of language. Punnery surprises us by flouting the law of nature that pretends that two things cannot occupy the same space at the same time. Punnery is an exercise of the mind at being concise. Punnery is a rewording experience.

Let's start by cooking up a punderful menu for Halloween. I know you won't be able to resist goblin up this full-corpse meal. Bone appetit!

Grains

Ghost Toasties   Scream of Wheat
Pentagram Crackers   Brain Muffins
   with Poisonbury Jam

Entrees

Hungarian Ghoul Ash   Frank 'n' Stein
Halloweenie   Black Catfish
Stake Sandwitch   Littleneck Clams
Warlocks and Bagels,   Grave-y
   with Scream Cheese

Side Dishes

Spook-ghetti   Deviled Eggs
Artichoke   Skullions
Scarrots   Ghost Liver Paté

Fruits

Adam's Apples   Nectarines

Desserts

I Scream   Boobury Pie Boo

Meringue   Ghoul Whip

Terrormisu   Ladyfingers

Ghoulda Cheese   Monster Cheese

Beverages

Ghoul Aid   Coffin with Scream

Zombie   Apple Spider

What do you get when you drop
a pumpkin?
Squash.

What's the favorite food of
mathematicians?
Pumpkin pi.

How can you help a Jack-o'-lantern
stop smoking?
Make him wear a pumpkin patch.

What do you call a yokel living on a farm?
A country pumpkin.

How do predatory canines find their way
around at night?
They carry jackal lanterns.

How did Mr. Hyde celebrate Halloween?
With a Jekyll lantern.

In Ireland, celebrants of Halloween carved out the insides of turnips and lit them with embers to represent the souls of the dead. The Irish brought this custom with them to America, only replacing turnips with the more abundant pumpkins, which had been grown here for more than 5,000 years. From pumpkins they began to create jack-o'-lanterns, and the custom spread.

The Irish tell a story about a notorious drunkard and trickster named Jack. He could not enter heaven because he was a miser, and he was unable to enter hell because he had played practical jokes on the devil. The devil gave him a single ember to light his way through the frigid darkness. Jack placed the hot coal inside a hollowed-out turnip to keep it glowing longer and was left to walk the earth until Judgment Day with his "Jack's lantern."

In honor of the seasonal pumpkin, let's celebrate some words that have one thing in common. They all end with the letters K-I-N. Provide the missing letters for each word defined:

1. Jack-o'-lantern material   _ _ _ _kin
2. Small fellow along the
   Yellow Brick Road   _ _ _ _ _kin
3. Lip wiper   _ _ _kin
4. Model of the human body   _ _ _ _kin
5. Related or similar   _kin
6. Awkward country fellow   _ _ _ _kin
7. NFL ball   _ _ _ _kin

Now step up to much rarer words that end in K-I-N:

8. Smooth twill suiting fabric _ _ _ _ _ _kin
9. Hip-length sleeveless jacket   _ _ _kin
10. Thick, blunt needle or dagger   _ _ _kin
11. Thick-soled, laced boot   _ _ _ _kin
12. Wooden tub or bucket   _ _ _kin
13. Spike of tightly clustered
    flowers   _ _ _kin
14. Individual baking dish   _ _ _ _kin
15. Small earthenware pot   _ _ _kin

Using the definitions as clues, identify the following words that begin with the letters K-I-N:

16. Considerate   kin _
17. Monarch   kin _
18. Class for children   kin _ _ _ _ _ _ _ _ _
19. To light a fire   kin _ _ _
20. Tight curl   kin _
21. Far out, eccentric   kin _ _

22. Relating to movement   kin _ _ _ _
23. Study of movement   kin _ _ _ _ _ _ _ _
24. Archaic plural of cow   kin_
25. Picture tube   kin _ _ _ _ _

Answers

1. pumpkin 2. munchkin 3. napkin 4. manikin
5. akin 6. bumpkin 7. pigskin

8. sharkskin 9. jerkin 10. bodkin 11. bushkin
12. firkin 13. catkin 14. ramekin 15. pipkin

16. kind 17. king 18. kindergarten 19. kindle
20. kink 21. kinky 22. kinetic 23. kinesiology
24. kine 25. kinescope

11

A Ghost Graduate Course

✻

Halloween was brought to America in the 1840s by Irish immigrants fleeing their country's potato famine. At that time, the favorite pranks in New England included tipping over outhouses and unhinging fence gates. According to the Dauphin County Library System, in 1921 Anoka, Minnesota, celebrated the first official city-wide observation of Halloween with carved pumpkins, a costumed square dance, and two parades. After that, it didn't take Halloween long to go nationwide. New York started celebrating in 1923 and Los Angeles in 1925.

The folklore of witches, ghosts, and cats in Halloween celebrations originates with the Druids. The Druids were an order of priests in ancient Gaul and Britain who believed that ghosts, spirits, fairies, witches, and elves came out on Halloween to harm people. They thought that cats had once been human beings but were changed as punishment for their evil deeds. Sharpen your pun cells now, and please join in some punnery about our favorite denizens of Halloween lore—ghosts, skeletons, witches, and monsters.

The spirited Halloween ball was a site for soirees. The spirit moved hundreds of specters from ghost to ghost to travel to the gala event. The ghosts danced sheet to sheet to some haunting melodies and boo-gied into the night. When the band wasn't playing from its sheet music, the ghostly revelers sang scare-ee-okee.

One of the apparitions was dressed in red and green. He was a Christmas wraith. Another came dressed up in a badly torn sheet. He was a holy terror. The women wore mas-scare-a, and their children came dressed up in white pillowcases.

Unfortunately, not a single skeleton attended the banquet. They had no body to go with, they didn't have the stomach for it, and they had no guts.

A number of the ghosts raised their goblets of boos as ghost toasts to dampen the spirits. As they became increasingly drunk and disorderly, one of the specters observed, "Just like when he was alive working as a bicycle mechanic, the bartender got the spooks too tight."

Some of these high spirits made overtures to the females present to accompany them elsewhere. Noting this, one of the matronly chaperoning angels warned a pretty winged novice in her charge: "You may partake of the punch, or even the nectars of the bar, but stay away from the Djinn and Chthonics. You may think you're famous, but you're just a bunch of nobodies."

The X-Files staff wished to take a picture of one of the ghosts at the Halloween ball. Because the event took place during darkest night, they decided to use flash photography. The ghost agreed to have its picture taken, but the photographer couldn't get the flash to work. The spirit was willing but the flash was weak. As a result, all *The X-Files* staff was able to develop was the Prints of Darkness.

Baby ghosts are often sent to dayscare centers where they play hide and shriek and peek-aboo. Their mothers advise them: "Don't spook until you're spooken to," "Put your boos and shocks on," and "Don't forget to boo-ckle your sheet belt." "Don't forget to say, 'How do you boo, sir or madam?'" If they don't obey, the trans-parents make the little ones ghost stand in a corner.

What's a ghost's favorite breakfast cereal?
*Ghost Toasties covered with evaporated
milk. (Isn't that a cereal killer?)*

Favorite singer:
Awraitha Franklin.

Favorite song:
"Ghost Riders in the Sky."

Favorite daytime talk show host:
Phantom of the Oprah.

Favorite cosmetic:
Vanishing cream.

Favorite religion:
Boo-dism.

Favorite children's games:
*Hide and go shriek, peekaboo,
and phantomime.*

Favorite children's toy:
A haunted doll house.

Favorite children's clothing:
Boo jeans.

Favorite amusement rides:
The scare-ousel, the moan-o-rail,
and the roller ghoster.

Favorite exercise machine:
The scare-master.

Favorite invention:
The elevator. It's guaranteed to
lift the spirits.

Favorite vacation retreats:
Mali-boo, the Scare-ibbean,
and Boo-da-pest.

Now that the ghost is clear, it's time for some spook-tacular, spirited puns about ghosts. You have more than a ghost of a chance of avoiding boo-boos and coming up with the right answers.

How does an exorcist keep in shape?
He rides an exorcycle.

What happens when you fire
your exorcist?
You get ex-spelled and repossessed.

What do you call a chicken that haunts
your house?
The poultrygeist.

What do you call a ghost hanging around
Santa's Workshop?
A North Poletergiest

What kind of horse does a ghost ride?
A night mare.

Why was the ghost surprised when his
girlfriend showed up for their date at
11:00 p.m.?
He didn't ex-specter until midnight.

What do you call a ghost who haunts
small hotels?
An inn specter.

Why are ghosts musical?
Because they like haunting melodies.

Where do Native American ghosts
hang out?
At the Happy Haunting Grounds.

What do you get when you cross Bambi
with a ghost?
Bamboo.

What do you get if you cross fake choco-
late with the ghost of an elk?
Carob-boo.

What do you use to get into a haunted
house?
A spook key.

Why did the game warden arrest the
ghost?
He didn't have a haunting license.

What do you call the ghost of an insect?
A bugaboo.

What do you call a ghost that sits in the picture window of a haunted house?
A window shade.

Why does an elevator make ghosts happy?
Because it lifts the spirits.

What do you call a ghostbuster?
A spooksperson.

Have you heard about the ghost who haunted a bell tower and disguised himself as one of the bells?
He was a doppelgonger.

What do spooks call their navy?
The Ghost Guard.

Where do ghosts go shopping?
In boo-tiques.

Who was the most famous ghost detective?
Sherlock Moans.

What do you call the ghosts of
dead turkeys?
Gobblins.

What happens when a ghost haunts a
theater?
The actors get stage fright.

Where do cowboy goblins live?
In ghost towns.

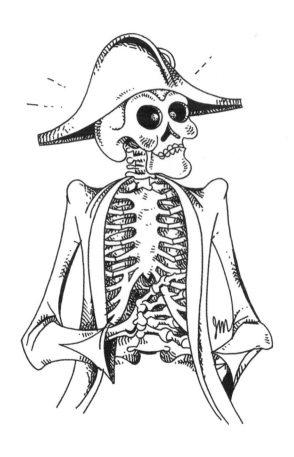

⚐⚐⚐
Funny Bones

❋

It's time to bone up on skeletons. These riddles and jokes about skeletons are guaranteed to tickle your skeletal funny bone:

What's a skeleton's favorite food?
Spare ribs.

Favorite historical figure:
Napoleon Bone-apart.

Favorite fictional detective:
Sherlock Bones.

Favorite comedian:
Red Skeleton.

Best subjects in school:
Anatomy. Bonehead English.

Favorite musical instrument:
The trombone.

How do you unlock a haunted house?
With a skeleton key.

What do you call a skeleton who goes
outside in winter with no hat on?
A numb skull.

Why is there no music at a church for
skeletons?
There aren't any organs.

Why didn't the skeleton exercise
his body?
*He was a lazy bones, and his
heart wasn't in it.*

What's worse than a vampire with
tooth decay?
A skeleton with arthritis.

Who was the famous female skeleton
who rode naked on a horse?
Lady Cadaver.

Where do skeletons eat lunch?
At the cadaver-teria.

What's the scariest job in the world?
The graveyard shift with a skeleton crew.

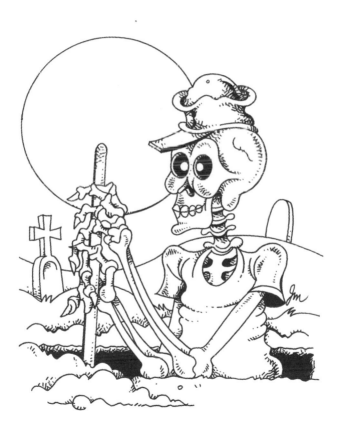

When does a skeleton laugh?
When something tickles his funny bone.

If you want to deliver mail to skeletons, try the bony express. Otherwise, the mail will end up at the dead-letter office.

And as skeletons say to their friends who are going on cruises, "Bone voyage!"

IV

Lifestyles of the Witch and Famous

Halloween is also the time for witchful thinking:

A young man was smitten by a lovely young lady. Although she was friendly to him, she did not share his romantic feelings. He decided to get some help. He approached the local witch group and asked for a love potion to slip to the reluctant lass.

The witches informed him that their new approach to witchcraft was to be kinder and gentler in their practice. Slipping potions to unsuspecting people was not ethical. They suggested a passive method that might work. The young man was sent on his way with a bottle containing thirty capsules. He was to bury one in the girl's yard each night until they were all gone.

A month later he returned to see the witches and told them that he and the girl were engaged to wed. He was ecstatic and wanted to know how the spell had worked. The witches explained to him that "Nothin' says lovin' like somethin' from the coven, and pills buried says it best."

Witches are flying sorcerers who operate a fly-by-night operation. They're so funny that every time they look in a mirror it cracks up.

On Halloween, they swoop through the air like scareplanes. When they break the sound barrier, you hear a sonic broom.

I tried to join a coven, but the doors warlocked. That's because there had just been a panty raid on the coven. It was an embarrassment of witches.

To make themselves attractive, witches go to the boo-ty parlor to purchase some scare spray and mass-scare-a. Then they hop on their brooms and sweep through the Halloween skies. They avoid riding their brooms when they're angry because they tend to fly off the handle. If their broom happens to break, they witch-hike—or they call broom service.

Once upon a time, two witches moved in together as broommates. Born after World War II, they were a couple of baby broomers. Their two brooms considered getting married, but they hadn't even swept together.

A little-known fact is that witches themselves actually go trick-or-treating. One witch draped herself with several strings of blinking Christmas-tree bulbs. She was a lights witch.

When the witches' pet spiders put on a production of *Pirates of Penzance*, the arachnid audience went wild as they started to sing, "When the foeman bares his steel, tarantula, tarantula!" Ultimately, all witches hope to be in the movies so they can win Academy A-warts.

What do you call the claim that witches have warts?
An ugly broomer.

Who is the author of this book?
Witch-ard Lederer.

What do you call an insect witch?
A coven-ant.

What has six legs and flies?
A witch and her cat on a broomstick.

What was the witch's favorite subject in school?
Spelling.

Why do witches often attend medical school?
So they can become witch doctors.

Where do witches go to get their hair done?
The ugly pallor.

What happens when witches are born as identical twins?
You can't tell which witch is which.

What brand of underwear do witches prefer?
Fruit of the Broom.

When the witch said, "Abradacabra," nothing happened. She's a hopeless speller.

One witch told another witch, "I want one of those new computers that has a spell checker."

Why did the witches' team lose the baseball game?
Their bats flew away.

What do you call a witch who lives at the beach?
A sand witch.

Who is the most famous witch detective?
Warlock Holmes.

What do you call a magic snake that keeps
witches away from your house?
A witch shield viper.

How do witches tell time?
On their witch watches.

What activity do witches love?
Witch arts and witch crafts.

How do you make a witch start scratch-
ing herself?
You take away her "w."

Have you heard about the witch who
contracted a skin disease from her pet?
She went from bat to warts.

In addition to Broomhilda, what cartoon
character is a favorite of witches?
Daddy Warlocks.

When is it bad luck to see a black cat?
When you're a mouse.

Once upon a time in England, a very mean witch was terrorizing the local population, who finally went to the resident wizard to see what could be done about her. The wizard gave them a potion that would turn the witch into a statue. The townspeople managed to put the potion in the witch's food. When she found out about this she turned green with rage, but it was too late, and the potion worked as expected.

The jubilant population had a big celebration and parade, and placed the petrified witch in a park as a public example. Pretty soon, people discovered that the witch had been frozen in a position that made her a perfect sundial, and they started using her to tell the time of day. The custom grew, and even today people often refer to Mean Green Witch Time.

✹

V

Word Prey in a Jugular Vein

Three vampires went into a bar and sat down. A buxom barmaid came over to take their orders. The vampires tried to be neck romancers, so they batted their eyes and flirted with her by telling her how much they liked her blood type. But she rebuffed them with the reply "O negative" and asked, "And what would you, er, gentlemen like tonight?"

The first vampire said, "I'll have a mug of blood."
The second vampire said, "I'll have a mug of blood."
The third vampire shook his head at his companions and said, "I'll have a glass of plasma."
The barmaid called out to the bartender, "Two bloods and a blood light!"

Then they all toasted each other by shouting, "This blood's for you!"

Vampires love to drink blood because they find it thicker than water. In fact, we know a vampire who was fired as night watchman at a blood bank. They caught him drinking on the job, thus making too many unauthorized withdrawals. And he took too many coffin breaks.

Long ago, vampires sailed to the United States in blood vessels and set up their own terror-tories. Many of them settled in the Vampire State, and others went west and became batboys for the Colorado Rockies' Horror Picture Show. Other vampires became umpires: Bats are attracted to other bats.

Some vampires went on to college and earned a place in Phi Batta Cape-a. Others perfected their skills at sucking blood by attending law school.

Vampires from all over the world gather each fall deep in the forests of Transylvania to renew their commitment to their calling. Here in their neck of the woods they sit around the vamp-fire and reverently view the scroll, writ-

ten and signed in blood, that contains their history and lists their rites and responsibilities. Then, at midnight, they stand at attention and swear allegiance to the Draculation of Vein Dependence and the Bill of Frights.

The most famous of all vampires is, of course, Count Dracula, the notorious neckrophiliac. He grew up as a spoiled bat and can be a real pain in the neck, but he can get under your skin. Even if he pays for dinner, he'll still put the bite on you.

Dracula once fell in love at first fright with the girl necks door. All she had to do was bat her eyes, and he'd give his eyeteeth to be with her. So she became his vein squeeze. She was six feet tall, and Dracula loves to suck up to women. But he's remained a bat-chelor his whole life because he always finds out that his sweetie isn't his blood type. His love affairs are all in vein. Anytime he courts another vampire, they end up at each other's throats, even if they just go out for a bite.

Any mortal woman to whom Dracula is attracted soon realizes that life with him will be an unfailingly draining experience, so she's not likely to stick her neck out for him. It's hard to get a good night's sleep with him because of the terrible coffin.

Moreover, Dracula isn't a very attractive fellow, in large part because he can't see himself in the bat room mirror and so is unable to brush his teeth, comb his hair, or tie his tie. This causes bat breath and the disease Dracula fears most—tooth decay. The fiend went to the dentist to correct his bite, but he still ended up with false teeth, which for him are new-fangled devices that, like Dracula himself, come out at night.

Dracula finds his victims in any neck of the woods. He just hates it when they try to cross him. Whenever the police come after him, the Count simply explains that he is a law-a-biting citizen. He loves the deep plots and grave setting of a cemetery, especially when the temperature rises above ninety degrees. Dracula often sighs, "There's nothing like a cold bier on a hot day." Actually, on a hot day Dracula has to apply gobs of sunscream. Sometimes the Count has to wait interminably to emerge from his coffin. To him it seems that the sun never sets on the brutish vampire.

Among Dracula's favorite songs are
*"You're So Vein" and "Fangs for the
Mammary. "*

His favorite TV show:
"Nip at Night."

His favorite television set:
A big-scream plasma TV.

His favorite roles in film:
The bit parts.

His favorite publisher:
William Randolph Hearse.

His favorite comic-book character:
Batman.

His favorite magazine:
Bleeders Digest. (It has great circulation.)

His favorite brand of facial tissue:
Kleenex.

His favorite dog:
The bloodhound.

His favorite animal:
*The giraffe. (There's so much
neck to gnaw on.)*

His least favorite insect:
*Mosquitoes. (They're too much
competition.)*

His favorite cars:
*The bloodmobile and the
Batmobile (especially for speeding
along a major artery).*

His favorite book:
"The Rise and Fall of the Roman Vampire."

His favorite sports:
Batminton and casketball.

His favorite children's game:
Hide and go suck.

His least favorite word game:
Crosswords.

His least favorite card game:
High-stakes poker.

His favorite hobby:
Casket-weaving.

His least favorite charity:
The Red Cross.

His favorite circus act:
The jugulars.

His favorite bodies of water:
Lake Eerie and the Dead Sea.

His favorite holiday:
Fangsgiving.

His favorite food:
Cape-on.

His favorite candy:
An all-day sucker.

His favorite drink:
De-coffin-ated coffee.

His favorite dance:
The fangdango.

Dracula's favorite barbecue meal is Hungarian ghoul ash. His least favorite food is a stake sandwich. That's why vampire parents tell their vampire children at an early age, "Whatever else you do, NEVER run with a wooden stake in your hands. Remember, your life's at stake." Also: "Eat your meal before it clots" and "Always bite the hand that feeds you." Even with this sound advice, vampire children can become spoiled bats and drive their parents batty.

Now here are some puns that you can really sink your teeth into. I'll have even more for you necks time.

What's the first thing that vampire children learn at school?
The alpha-bat.

Did you hear about the vampire poet?
Things went from bat to verse.

What did the vampire do when he saw a funeral procession?
He took a turn for the hearse.

What did one vampire say to another as
they passed the mortuary?
"Let's stop in for a cold one."

What do you get when you cross Dracula
with Long John Silver?
You get a vampirate.

What do vampires take for a sore throat?
Coffin drops.

Did you hear about the vampire's arithmetic homework assignment?
It was a blood count.

What's the difference between an optimist and a vampire killer?
One counts his blessings, and the other blesses his counts.

Why was the vampire expelled from school?
For failing the blood test.

Did you hear about the vampire in jail?
He was in a blood cell.

Why did the vampire cross the road?
His teeth couldn't let go of the chicken's neck.

Why did the vampire wrestler get so many compound fractures?
Because people never give a sucker an even break.

If two vampires had a race, who
would win?
Neither. They'd finish neck and neck.

Why was Dracula banished from Serbia?
Because he slobbered on Milosevic.

Did you hear about the Native
American vampire?
He was a full-blooded Indian.

Who went to the vampires'
family reunion?
All of the blood relations.

Who does Dracula get letters from?
His fang club.

Why did the vampire go to the
orthodontist?
To improve his bite.

Vampire teacher: How do you
spell *coffin?*
Little Dracula: K-A-U-G-H-E-N.
Vampire teacher: That's the worst *coffin*
spell I have ever heard.

A vampire joined the police force so he could learn the correct way to conduct a stake out.

How can you spot a vampire jockey?
He always wins by a neck.

Above all, Dracula hopes that his victims won't cross him.

"I've just killed Dracula," said Tom Swift painstakingly.

Have you read the other new book, about a cross-dressing vampire?
It's called "Dragula."

Where do they cremate seductive women?
On vamp pyres.

Where does Count Dracula usually eat his lunch?
At the casketeria.

If Tony Bennett were a vampire, what would his song be?
"I Left Her Heart in San Francisco."

Did you hear about the unsuccessful vampire hunter?
He tried to kill a vampire by driving a pork chop through its heart because steaks were too expensive.

Knock, knock.
Who's there?
Ivan.
Ivan who?
Ivan to drink your blood.

Or, as Dracula said to his apprentice, "We could do with some new blood around here."

Why are there so many vampires in Hollywood?
Somebody has to play the bit parts.

How did the race between two vampires end?
They finished neck and neck.

What is the motto of the vampire baby boom generation?
There's a sucker born every minute.

Why did the vampire wrestler get so
many compound fractures?
*Because people never give a sucker an
even break.*

Why did the vampire go into a
fast-food restaurant?
For a quick bite.

How many vampires does it take to
change a light bulb?
None. Vampires prefer the dark.

Vampires don't like to be crossed, but they
often are, as the following curious clonings
will show:

What do you get if you cross a vampire
and a vegetarian?
*Something that tries to get blood from a
turnip.*

What do you get when you cross a snow-
man with a vampire?
Frostbite.

What do you get when you cross Dracula
and a fish?
Cape Cod.

What do you get when you cross
Dracula and a duck?
Count Drakeula or Count Duckula.

What do you get when you cross
Dracula and a dog?
*Something whose bite is worse than
its bark.*

What do you get when you cross a vampire with a large antlered animal?
Vamoose!

Now it's time to say goodbye to Dracula
and his batty friends: "So long, suckers!"

VI
Puns That Keep Us in Stitches

Halloween is a time when we conjure up visions of all manner of ghoulies and ghosties and long-leggety beasties. Along with Dracula, the most popular of these grotesques is the Frankenstein monster, not to be confused with Dr. Victor Frankenstein, his creator. Victor was a direct descendant of the man who harnessed electricity by flying a kite: Benjamin Frankenstein.

Despite his evil reputation, Dr. Victor Frankenstein actually had a good sense of humor; he kept his monster in stitches. Frankenstein was also a philanthropist because he founded the first organ donor program—a dead giveaway to his good heart. He also loved his dog—a black Lab, of course. And

when the monster rose from the table and spat on the ground, the proud doctor exclaimed, "It's saliva! It's saliva!"

Doctor Frankenstein's assistant, Igor, was also a doctor and together they were a pair o' docs. When they decided to stop making monsters, Igor found a new job at an auto dealership as parts manager.

Even though Frankenstein's monster's twisted body strikes us as shocking and revolting, he had his heart in the right place. In fact, he once had a ghoul friend to take out for a frank 'n' stein. He just couldn't resistor. Now he has a new ghoul friend named Endora. He'd previously dated a lady scarecrow but went from rags to witches.

Sensitive fellow that old Zipperneck was, he also developed an identity crisis. He kept hoping that he had a mummy and dead-y, but they never appeared. So he went to a psychiatrist to see if he had a screw loose. One day, he decided to take the five o'clock train. But the authorities made him give it back. Actually, the townspeople came to love Frankenstein's monster; to a man they carried a torch for him.

Ultimately, the government re-monsterated Dr. Frankenstein and sued for custody of his creation. The bureaucrats wanted to donate the monster's body parts to medical schools, but their plan was a dead give-away.

Since both parties demanded sole custody in the Frankenstein lawsuit, the judge called for a sword-of-Solomon socket wrench and ruled an equitable split: The government was granted permission to raise the creature's grotesque body, while Victor reared its ugly head.

VII
More Movie Monsters

Almost as central in our popular culture as Frankenstein is the image of the werewolf. Did you know that werewolves love to eat sheep because they can dine and floss at the same time?

One day, a fellow went to a clinic and complained, "Doctor, doctor! I feel like I'm a werewolf." The doctor replied, "Have a seat and comb your face." Then the patient became an aware wolf.

Wolfman lived in a werehouse in San Francisco. When he felt mischievous, he would moon at the bay. Afterwards, he moved to a larger community of werewolves—Howlywood—where he auditioned for bit parts. He didn't have much luck and had to move into a small room in the Howl-a-Day Inn.

His vulpine body caused him to contract irritable howl syndrome and to soil his clothes frequently, so he had to visit the Laundromat almost every day. He became a washin' werewolf. He also took up clay-spinning as a hobby and became a hairy potter.

One evening, Wolfman came home from a long day at the office.

"How was work, dear?" his wife asked.

"Listen! I don't want to talk about work!" he shouted.

"Okay. Would you like to sit down and eat a nice home-cooked meal?" she asked nicely.

"I'm not hungry!" he snarled. "I don't wanna eat! Is that all right with you? Can I come home from work and just do my own thing without you forcing food down my throat? Huh!"

Then Wolfman started growling and throwing things around the apartment in a titanic rage.

Looking out the window, his wife saw a full moon and said to herself, "Well, I guess it must be that time of the month."

Also enshrined in the pantheon of famous movie monsters is the Invisible Man. Don't bother inviting the Invisible Man to your Halloween party. He won't show up. Sometimes he makes excuses, but they're all transparent. You can see right through them.

Invisible's mother and father were also invisible. They were trans-parents. He had an invisible girlfriend who used a lot of vanishing cream. Ultimately, Invisible's girlfriend preferred seeing other men. As a child, Invisible wasn't much to look at. When he was a teenager, he seldom hung out with his friends. There was simply too much disappear pressure. Whenever he tried to make a point with his friends, they just said, "I don't see where you're coming from." Ultimately, the Invisible Man went crazy. You know, out of sight; out of mind.

Recently, a number of movies featuring the Mummy have drawn enormous audiences who watch the action in Horrorscope. You could brand these movies Fruit of the Tomb.

The Mummy's mummy was also an entertainer—a famous gauza stripper, although the family kept that under wraps. She feels it's a good investment to stand in front of a mirror because it doubles your mummy. Off the silver screen the Mummy isn't very popular with the other monsters. They think he's egotistical because he's all wrapped up in himself. Being interested in band ages, he loves music, his favorite style being wrap. He also plays a mean trumpet. Put him in front of an audience, and he'll toot uncommon.

He would love to take a vacation at the Dead Sea, but he's afraid that he'll relax and unwind too much. That's one way that mummies get a bad wrap. Moreover, he's got to get his pyramid exterminated because it's infested with cryptics.

As the sign in the Egyptian funeral home says: "Satisfaction guaranteed or your mummy back!"

As one mummy said to the other, "It's a wrap. I'll B.C.ing you!"

✻

VIII
Ghoulishness

❀

You've heard of Quasimodo, haven't you?—not the real modo, but the quasi-modo, not the quarterback of Notre Dame, not the halfback of Notre Dame, not the fullback of Notre Dame, but the hunchback of Notre Dame. You know, he was the one who, when people told him that he was ugly, got all bent out of shape. At any rate, having grown too old to ring the bell in the cathedral tower, Quasimodo ran an ad in the local newspaper for a replacement.

An armless man appeared at Quasimodo's door, and the ring-master asked him, "Are you here for the job of bell ringer?"

"Yes, I am."

"But how can you ring the bell when you have no arms?"

"That's easy," answered the man disarmingly. "I may lack arms, but I possess an extremely tough skull. I simply run at the bell and strike it with my forehead. The tone produced is absolutely exquisite."

"All right," conceded Quasimodo and, on a hunch, hired the fellow.

The man ascended the spiral staircase, climbed into the bell tower, ran at the bell, and struck it with his forehead, indeed making a lovely clang. Alas, though, the bell swung back pendularly, smashed into the poor chap, and knocked him out of the tower. He splatted on the cobblestones far below.

When the police arrived at the scene, an officer asked, "Mr. Quasimodo, do you know this man?"

"Yes, I do," answered Quasi. "He was an employee of mine."

"For our records, please give us his name." Quasimodo furrowed his brow. "I don't know his name, but his face rings a bell."

Shortly thereafter, Quasimodo placed a second ad in the paper asking for new bell-ringing applicants. A second gentlemen appeared who looked exactly like the first, including the prominent lack of appendages in the upper torso area.

Quasimodo asked the new man, "Are you here for the position of bell-ringer?"

"Yes, I am."

"Then I have two questions for you. First, am I wrong or do you look exactly like another fellow who was recently in my employ and who came to a tragic end by jumping to a conclusion?"

"That man was my older brother," replied the applicant. "Indeed, many people have remarked that I look just like him."

"You look so much like him," Quasimodo went on, "that you too exhibit a prominent lack of appendages in the upper torso area. How do you propose to ring the bell?"

"Easy. Like my brother, I too have an exceedingly tough forehead, which I use to ring the bell, but I am more agile than my brother, and I have learned to get out of the way of the bell's backswing."

"Fine," sighed Quasimodo with relief. "You may start immediately."

The second gentleman mounted the spiral staircase, climbed up to the tower, and ran headlong into the bell, producing as exquisite a tone as had his brother. As the bell swayed back toward him, he deftly stepped aside and avoided getting clobbered by the return swing.

Alas, though, three nights later, the new bell ringer got stinking drunk. He staggered up the spiral staircase, lurched toward the bell, and struck it with his forehead. As he stood there swaying in his drunken stupor, the bell swung back and knocked him out of the tower and onto the cobblestones below.

Again the police arrived. "Do you know this man, Mr. Quasimodo?"

"Yes, he too was an employee of mine," answered the hunchback.

"May we have his name, please?"

"I don't know his name either, but he's a dead ringer for his brother."

Now it's time to sharpen your pun cells with some riddles and jokes about monsters other than Frankenstein, Wolfman, the Invisible Man, the Mummy, and Quasimodo. These monsters are so scary that just looking at them makes you soil your underwear. With fiends like these, who needs enemas?

Who are the monsters' favorite singers?
Robert Ghoulet and Bury Man in Low.

Favorite play:
"Romeo and Ghouliet."

Favorite TV shows:
"Ghouligan's Island" and "The Broody Bunch."

Favorite song:
"Ghouls Just Want to Have Fun."

Favorite country western song:
"I Fall To Pieces."

Favorite bedtime story:
"Ghoul Deluxe and the Three Scares."

Favorite games:
Swallow the leader, corpse and robbers, hide and go shriek, and cryptic crossword puzzles.

Favorite flower:
Mourning gory.

Favorite brand of underwear:
Zom-B.V.D.'s and Fruit of the Tomb.

Favorite hockey position:
Ghoulie.

Favorite illustrator:
Edward Gorey.

Favorite stuffed animal:
The deady bear.

Favorite foods:
Creep suzettes and Munster cheese.

Favorite presidential candidate:
Al Gore.

Favorite expression:
"Eat your heart out."

Least favorite place in the home:
The living room.

Once upon a slime, a ghoul fell in love with
a mummy. Alas, the ghoul did not know much

about proper care of mummies, and in a couple of weeks the mummy began to unravel and disintegrated. The moral of the story: A ghoul and his mummy are soon parted.

What happened to the monster that took
the five o'clock train home?
They made him give it back.

Why did the monster eat the caboose?
Because the locomotive told him,
"Choo, choo!"

What is a monster's normal eye sight?
20-20-20-20.

What monster is the best dancer?
The Boogie Man.

Why do they put fences around
cemeteries?
Because everybody's dying to get in there.

How do ghouls celebrate Halloween?
They go out and paint the town dead.

Why do you always find ghouls and
demons together?
Because demons are a ghoul's best friend.

What did the ghoul buy for
his ghoulfiend?
A set of his and hearse pajamas.

What did the ghoul shout when the diggers wanted to use his gravesite?
"You'll do it over my dead body!"

How does a ghoul begin a formal letter?
"Tomb it may concern."

Who brings up a baby ghoul?
Its mummy and deady.

Where do ghouls live?
On dead-end streets.

Where do ghouls get their mail?
At the ghost office in the dead letter department.

Why do zombies play cards in a cemetery?
Just in case they have to dig up another player.

What happened to the monster children who ate all their vegetables?
They gruesome.

Why didn't the zombie win his lawsuit?
He didn't have a leg to stand on.

What is the favorite brand of
toothpaste for little devils?
Imp-U-Dent.

What did the monster Superman say to
the dead Lois Lane?
"Shall we sleep in the Kryptonite?"

Knock knock.
Who's there?
Zombies.
Zombies who?
Zombies make honey and zombies don't.

What do monsters say when something is
really neat?
"Ghoul!"

What kind of a car does Satan drive?
A Coupe Devil.

Did you hear about the seriously
ill zombie?
He's in grave condition.

Why was the zombie kicked out of the
gravediggers' glee club?
Because he couldn't carry a tomb.

How do the corpses in graveyards send
messages to each other?
Crypt-o-grams.

Why did the doctor tell the zombie to get
some rest?
He was dead on his feet.

What do you call a zombie
door-to-door salesman?
A dead ringer.

Whom did the zombie invite to his party?
Anyone he could dig up.

What did the wicked chicken lay?
Deviled eggs.

What do you get if you cross a Scottish
locksmith, a bird, and Frankenstein?
A lock nest monster.

Is it okay for a zombie to eat fried
chicken with his fingers?
*No, the fingers should be eaten
separately.*

What's the difference between a lame
sailor and a monster?
*One's a gob hobblin' and the other's a
hobgoblin.*

✳

Acknowledgments

�֎

Many of the puns in this book have been circulating for years in cyberspace and print. It is exceedingly difficult to uncover the names of their authors because, as with all folklore, the material surfaces in various forms and with different names attached.

To the best of my knowledge the following are authors of one or more of the gems in this book: Nick Brown, Paul Croft, Norman Gilbert, Gary Hallock, Lars Hanson, Jackie Holle, Stan Kegel, Gill Krebs, Cynthia MacGregor, Joseph Rosenbloom, Bill Stubbins, P. C. Swanson, Jess Symonds, Trinitty, Clynch Varnadore, and Randall Woodman.